Peter
Pedro *(peh-droh)*
Pierre *(p'yehr)*
Пётр *(pyoh-tr)*

Paul
Pablo *(pah-bloh)*
Paul *(pohl)*
Павел *(pahv-yehl)*

Elizabeth
Isabel *(ee-sah-behl)*
Elisabeth *(eh-lee-zah-beht)*
Елизавета *(yeh-lee-zah-vyeh-tah)*

George
Jorge *(hohr-heh)*
Georges *(zhohr-zhuh)*
Георгий *(gyeh-ohr-gee)*

Mary
María *(mah-ree-ah)*
Marie *(mah-ree)*
Мария *(mah-ree-yah)*

Catherine
Catalina *(kah-tah-lee-nah)*
Catherine *(kah-treen)*
Екатерина *(yeh-kah-tyeh-ree-nah)*

Susan
Susana *(soo-sah-nah)*
Suzanne *(sew-zahn)*
Сюзанна *(syoo-zahn-nah)*

John
Juan *(hooan)*
Jean *(zhahn)*
Иван *(ee-vahn)*

In School

IN SCHOOL

Learning in Four Languages
by Esther Hautzig
pictures by Nonny Hogrogian

The Macmillan Company • Collier-Macmillan Ltd., London

413
H
C
1971

30027000015914

*French, Spanish and Russian words and phonetics by the editorial staff of
Berlitz Publications, Inc.*

For my teachers—

Rachel Polak • Anna Semyonovna • Leo Gurko

The first day of school is very exciting.
In San Francisco or San Sebastián,
Cherbourg or Odessa,
children come to school
to study and learn
and to have fun, too.

Boys and girls are proud and happy,
and a little nervous,
as they say good-by to their parents.
It is time to meet their teacher,
see their classroom
and make new friends
in San Francisco or San Sebastián,
Cherbourg or Odessa.

school
escuela (ehs-_kweh_-lah)
école (eh-_kohl_)
школа (_shkoh_-lah)

boys
muchachos (moo-_chah_-chohs)
garçons (gahr-_sohng_)
мальчики (_mahl_-chee-kee)

parents
padres (_pah_-drehs)
parents (pah-_rahng_)
родители (rah-_dee_-tyeh-lee)

girls
niñas (_nee_-n'yahs)
jeunes filles (zhuhn _fee_-yuh)
девочки (_dyeh_-vahch-kee)

teacher
maestro (mah-_ehs_-troh)
professeur (proh-feh-_suhr_)
учитель (oo-_chee_-tyehl)

The teacher smiles and says hello.
She takes attendance.
Everyone listens as names of classmates,
and their own,
are called out in school
in San Francisco or San Sebastián,
Cherbourg or Odessa.

desk
escritorio *(ehs-kree-toh-r'yoh)*
bureau *(bew-roh)*
парта *(pahr-tah)*

class
clase *(klah-seh)*
classe *(klahs)*
класс *(klahs)*

schoolroom
aula *(ow-lah)*
salle de classe *(sahl duh klahs)*
класс *(klahs)*

notebooks
cuadernos *(kwah-dehr-nohs)*
cahiers *(kah-yeh)*
тетрадки *(tyeh-traht-kee)*

pupils
alumnos *(ah-loom-nohs)*
élèves *(eh-lehv)*
ученики *(oo-chee-nee-kee)*

The first lesson begins.
Everyone studies multiplication and division,
subtraction and addition.
Some children like arithmetic,
others do not, but everyone learns it
in San Francisco or San Sebastián,
Cherbourg or Odessa.

arithmetic
aritmética *(ah-reet-meh-tee-kah)*
arithmétique *(ah-ree-tmeh-teek)*
арифметика *(ah-reef-myeh-tee-kah)*

$$2 \times 2 = 4$$

multiplication
multiplicación *(mool-tee-plee-kah-th'yohn)*
multiplication *(mewl-tee-plee-kah-s'yohng)*
умножение *(oom-nah-zhyeh-nee-yeh)*

$$3\overline{)9}\ \ 3$$

division
división *(dee-vee-s'yohn)*
division *(dee-vee-z'yohng)*
деление *(dyeh-lyeh-nee-yeh)*

$$\begin{array}{r} 10 \\ -4 \\ \hline 6 \end{array}$$

subtraction
substracción *(soobs-trahk-th'yohn)*
soustraction *(soos-trahk-s'yohng)*
вычитание *(vih-chee-tah-nee-yeh)*

addition
suma *(soo-mah)*
addition *(ah-dee-s'yohng)*
сложение *(slah-zhyeh-nee-yeh)*

$$\begin{array}{r} 7 \\ +5 \\ \hline 12 \end{array}$$

When the arithmetic lesson is over
everyone is happy to have a music period.
Boys and girls sing and dance
and play many different instruments
in San Francisco or San Sebastián,
Cherbourg or Odessa.

music
música *(moo-see-kah)*
musique *(mew-zeek)*
музыка *(moo-zih-kah)*

dance
bailar *(by-lahr)*
danser *(dahn-seh)*
танцовать *(tahn-tseh-vahts)*

instrument
instrumento *(eens-troo-mehn-toh)*
instrument *(ehngs-trew-mahng)*
инструмент *(een-stroo-myehnt)*

sing
cantar *(kahn-tahr)*
chanter *(shahn-teh)*
петь *(pyehts)*

A science period comes next.
It is exciting to visit the science room,
to look through the microscope,
feed the animals, learn how plants grow
and perform experiments.

science
ciencia *(th'yehn-th'yah)*
science *(s'yahns)*
наука *(nah-oo-kah)*

experiment
experimento *(ehks-peh-ree-mehn-toh)*
épreuve *(eh-pruhv)*
опыт *(oh-piht)*

magnet

imán *(ee-mahn)*

aimant *(eh-mahng)*

магнит *(mahg-neet)*

During recess boys and girls
rush into the schoolyard.
They jump and run
and play different games
in San Francisco or San Sebastián,
Cherbourg or Odessa.

schoolyard
patio de recreo *(pah-tee-oh deh reh-kreh-oh)*
cour de récréation *(koor duh reh-kreh-ah-s'yohng)*
школьная площадка *(shkohl-nah-yah plah-shchaht-kah)*

ball
pelota *(peh-loh-tah)*
ballon *(bah-lohng)*
мяч *(myahch)*

jump
saltar *(sahl-tahr)*
sauter *(soh-teh)*
прыгать *(prih-gahts)*

run
correr *(koh-rrehr)*
courir *(koo-reer)*
бегать *(byeh-gahts)*

When they come back to the classroom
boys and girls work on their
reading, writing and spelling.
They learn the meaning of many new words
in English or Spanish,
French or Russian.

blackboard
pizarra *(pee-thah-rrah)*
tableau noir *(tah-bloh nwahr)*
доска *(dahs-kah)*

reading
lectura *(lehk-too-rah)*
lecture *(lehk-tewr)*
чтение *(chtyeh-nee-yeh)*

spelling
deletrear *(deh-leh-treh-ahr)*
orthographe *(ohr-toh-grahf)*
правописание *(prah-vah-pee-sah-nee-yeh)*

writing
escritura *(ehs-kree-too-rah)*
écriture *(eh-kree-tewr)*
писание *(pee-sah-nee-yeh)*

An art period comes next.
It is fun to work with colors.
Everyone paints what he likes
in San Francisco or San Sebastián,
Cherbourg or Odessa.

paint
pintar *(peen-tahr)*
peindre *(pehndr)*
красить *(khrah-seets)*

pictures
cuadros *(kwah-drohs)*
tableaux *(tah-bloh)*
картины *(kahr-tee-nih)*

artists
artistas *(ahr-tees-tahs)*
artistes *(ahr-teest)*
художники *(khoo-doh-zhnee-kee)*

colors
colores *(koh-loh-rehs)*
couleurs *(koo-luhr)*
краски *(krahs-kee)*

Everyone likes the school library.
There are so many books
about everything and everywhere
to read, look at and take home
in San Francisco or San Sebastián,
Cherbourg or Odessa.

library
biblioteca *(bee-blee-oh-<u>teh</u>-kah)*
bibliothèque *(bee-blee-oh-<u>tehk</u>)*
библиотека *(beeb-lee-ah-<u>tyeh</u>-kah)*

librarian
bibliotecario *(bee-blee-oh-teh-<u>kah</u>-ree-oh)*
bibliothécaire *(bee-blee-oh-teh-<u>kehr</u>)*
библиотекарь *(beeb-lee-ah-<u>tyeh</u>-kahr)*

books
libros *(<u>lee</u>-brohs)*
livres *(leevr)*
книги *(<u>knee</u>-gee)*

study
estudiar *(ehs-too-d'yahr)*
étudier *(eh-tew-d'yeh)*
учиться *(oo-cheet-syah)*

bookshelves
estantes *(ehs-tahn-tehs)*
rayons *(reh-yohng)*
книжные полки *(kneezh-nih-yeh pohl-kee)*

At the end of the day
boys and girls know their schoolroom,
their teacher and each other, too.
They have also learned how much there is to learn.

friends
amigos *(ah-mee-gohs)*
amis *(ah-mee)*
друзья *(drooz-yah)*

homework
tarea *(tah-reh-ah)*
devoir *(duh-vwahr)*
домашняя работа *(dah-mah-shnyah rah-boh-tah)*

The school day is over.
Everyone goes home
with happy news of the first day
in school in San Francisco or San Sebastián,
Cherbourg or Odessa.

Class dismissed!

¡La clase ha terminado! *(lah klah-seh ah tehr-mee-nah-doh)*

La classe est finie! *(lah klahs eh fee-nee)*

Урок окончен! *(oo-rohk ah-kohn-chehn)*

Additional Words

chalk	tiza _tee-thah_	craie _kreh_	мел _myehl_
Cherbourg	Cherburgo _chehr-boor-goh_	Cherbourg _shehr-boor_	Шербург _shyehr-boor_
coatrack	percha _pehr-chah_	portemanteau _pohrt-mahn-toh_	вешалка _vyeh-shahl-kah_
drum	tambor _tahm-bohr_	tambour _tahn-boor_	барабан _bah-rah-bahn_
English	inglés _een-glehs_	anglais _ahn-gleh_	английский _ahn-glee-skee_
French	francés _frahn-thehs_	français _frahn-seh_	французский _frahn-tsoo-skee_
games	juegos _hweh-gohs_	jeux _zhuh_	игры _ee-grih_
hat	sombrero _sohm-breh-roh_	chapeau _shah-poh_	шапка _shahp-kah_
learn	aprender _ah-prehn-dehr_	apprendre _ah-prahndr_	учиться _oo-chee-tsah_
mittens	mitones _mee-toh-nehs_	moufles _moof-luh_	варежки _vah-ryehsh-kee_
mouse	ratón _rah-tohn_	souris _soo-ree_	мышь _mihsh_

Odessa	Odesa	Odessa	Одесса
	oh-deh-sah	*oh-deh-sah*	*ah-dyeh-sah*
paintbrush	brocha	pinceau	кисть
	broh-chah	*pehng-soh*	*keests*
paper	papel	papier	бумага
	pah-pehl	*pah-pyeh*	*boo-mah-gah*
pen	pluma	plume	перо
	ploo-mah	*plewm*	*pyeh-roh*
pencil	lápiz	crayon	карандаш
	lah-peeth	*kreh-yohng*	*kah-rahn-dahsh*
plant	planta	plante	растение
	plahn-tah	*plahnt*	*rah-styeh-nee-yeh*
rabbit	conejo	lapin	кролик
	koh-neh-hoh	*lah-pehng*	*kroh-leek*
recess	descanso	récréation	каникулы
	dehs-kahn-soh	*reh-kreh-ah-s'yohng*	*kah-nee-koo-lih*
Russian	ruso	russe	русский
	roo-soh	*rews*	*roos-kee*
San Francisco	San Francisco	San Francisco	Сан Франциско
	sahn frahn-thees-koh	*sahn frahn-sees-koh*	*sahn frahn-tsees-koh*
San Sebastián	San Sebastián	Saint-Sébastien	Сан Себастиян
	sahn seh-bahs-tee-ahn	*sehng seh-bahs-t'yehng*	*sahn seh-bahs-tee-ahn*
Spanish	español	espagnol	испанский
	ehs-pah-n'yohl	*ehs-pah-n'yohl*	*ees-pahn-skee*

Russian Alphabet

А	а	ah as in arch	П	п	p as in pie
Б	б	b as in boy	Р	р	r as in porridge
В	в	v as in voice	С	с	s as in stay
Г	г	g as in good	Т	т	t as in toy
Д	д	d as in do	У	у	oo as in boot
Е	е	yeh as in yet	Ф	ф	f as in fix
Ё	ё	yoh as in yoyo	Х	х	kh as in huge
Ж	ж	zh as in pleasure	Ц	ц	ts as in let's go
З	з	z as in zero	Ч	ч	ch as in church
И	и	ee as in feet	Ш	ш	sh as in short
Й	й	y as in yeast	Щ	щ	shch as in borshch
К	к	k as in keep	Ъ	ъ	separation sign (')
Л	л	l as in luck	Ы	ы	ih as in a drawn-out is
М	м	m as in me	Ь	ь	soft sign (preceding consonant pronounced as if ee followed)
Н	н	n as in now			
О	о	oh as in often when stressed, closer to ah when unstressed	Э	э	eh as in empty
			Ю	ю	yoo as you
			Я	я	yah as in yard

413
H   c.1

Hautzig, Esther
In school

DATE DUE	BORROWER'S NAME	ROOM NUMBER
FEB 23	S. Kaplan	124
OCT 8 '76	B. Brisch	123
MAR 18 '7?	Roosevelt D	12
APR 1 '77	R. B...	124

                                         c.1
413   Hautzig, Esther
H   In school; learning in four languages;
         pictures by Nonny Hogrogian, Macmillan,
         1969.
         unp. illus.

         Depicts school activities in English
         French, Spanish and Russian vocabulary.